ST NICHOLAS CATHOLIC SCHOOL

30004749

S0-AVG-036

PROPERTY OF
ST. NICHOLAS SCHOOL LIBRARY
LOS ALTOS HILLS

IN THE PARK

IN THE PARK

An Excursion in Four Languages

by ESTHER HAUTZIG
Pictures by EZRA JACK KEATS

410
HAU

THE MACMILLAN COMPANY, NEW YORK
COLLIER-MACMILLAN LIMITED, LONDON

Copyright © Esther Hautzig 1968

Copyright © Ezra Jack Keats 1968

All rights reserved. No part of this book may be reproduced
or transmitted in any form or by any means, electronic or
mechanical, including photocopying, recording or by any
information storage and retrieval system, without permission
in writing from the Publisher.

The Macmillan Company, New York
Collier-Macmillan Canada, Ltd., Toronto, Ontario

Library of Congress catalog card number: 68-10067

Printed in the United States of America

FIRST PRINTING

Phonetics checked by the editorial staff of Berlitz Publications, Inc.

3117

For our David
who loves all parks

On a sunny day
Everyone goes to the park
In New York   or Paris,

Moscow

or Madrid.

It is nice in the park. So much to see and do. Such fun to visit. In New York

or Paris,

trees

arbres
ahrbr

деревья
d'yeh-r'yeh-v'yah

árboles
ahr-boh-lehs

squirrels

écureuils
eh-kew-roy

белки
b'yehl-kee

ardillas
ahr-dee-l'yahs

Moscow

or Madrid
A park has . . .

grass

herbe
ehrb

трава
trah-vah

hierba
yehr-bah

lampposts

réverbères
reh-vehr-behr

фонарные столбы
fah-nahr-nee-yeh stohl-bee

postes de la luz
pohs-tehs deh lah looth

rocks

rocs
rohk

скалы
skah-lee

rocas
roh-kahs

benches

bancs
bahng

скамьи
sk'ahm-yee

bancos
bahn-kohs

flowers

fleurs
fluhr

цветы
tsv'yeh-<u>tee</u>

flores
<u>floh</u>-rehs

playgrounds

cours de récréation
koor duh reh-kreh-ah-s'yohng

площадки для игры
plah-sh'<u>chahd</u>-kee dl'ya ee-<u>gree</u>

patios de recreo
<u>pah</u>-tee-ohs deh reh-<u>kreh</u>-oh

PROPERTY OF
ST. NICHOLAS SCHOOL LIBRARY
LOS ALTOS HILLS

monuments

monuments
moh-new-mahng

ПАМЯТНИКИ
pah-m'yaht-nee-kee

monumentos
moh-noo-mehn-tohs

pigeons

pigeons
pee-<u>zhohng</u>

голуби
<u>goh</u>-loo-bee

palomas
pah-<u>loh</u>-mahs

fountains

fontaines
fohn-<u>tehn</u>

фонтаны
fahn-<u>tah</u>-nee

fuentes
<u>fwehn-tehs</u>

Some parks have a zoo. In the zoo there are . . .

elephants

éléphants
eh-leh-<u>fahng</u>

слоны
slah-<u>nee</u>

elefantes
eh-leh-<u>fahn</u>-tehs

zebras

zèbres
zehb'r

зебры
z'<u>yeh</u>-bree

cebras
<u>theh</u>-brahs

hippopotamuses	penguins
hippopotames	**pingouins**
ee-poh-poh-<u>tahm</u>	pehn-<u>gwehng</u>
ГИППОПОТАМЫ	ПИНГВИНЫ
ghee-pah-pah-<u>tah</u>-mee	peeng-<u>vee</u>-nee
hipopótamos	**pingüinos**
ee-poh-<u>poh</u>-tah-mohs	pin-<u>gwee</u>-nohs

seals

phoques
fokk

ТЮЛЕНИ
t'you-l'yeh-nee

focas
foh-kahs

deer

cerfs
sehr

ОЛЕНИ
oh-l'yeh-nee

ciervos
s'yehr-vohs

foxes	bears
renards	**ours**
ruh-<u>nahr</u>	oorss
ЛИСИЦЫ	**медведи**
lee-<u>see</u>-tsee	myed-v'<u>yeh</u>-dee
zorros	**osos**
<u>thohr</u>-rohs	<u>oh</u>-sohs

In every park
In New York

or Paris,

kites

cerfs-volants
sehr voh-lahng

воздушные змеи
vahz-doo'sh-nee-yeh z'meh-ee

cometas
koh-meh-tahs

balls

balles
bahl

МЯЧИ
m'yah-chee

pelotas
peh-loh-tahs

Moscow

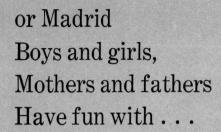

or Madrid
Boys and girls,
Mothers and fathers
Have fun with . . .

swings

balançoires
bah-lawn-<u>swahr</u>

качели
kah-ch'<u>yeh</u>-lee

columpios
koh-<u>loom</u>-p'yohs

slides

toboggans
toh-boh-<u>gahng</u>

горки
<u>gohr</u>-kee

resbaladeros
rehs-bal-ah-<u>deh</u>-rohs

bicycles

bicyclettes
bee-see-<u>kleht</u>

велосипеды
v'yeh-lah-see-p'yeh-dee

bicicletas
bee-thee-<u>kleh</u>-tahs

jump ropes

cordes à sauter
kohrd ah soh-<u>teh</u>

скакалки
sk'ah-<u>kahl</u>-kee

combas
<u>kohm</u>-bahs

scooters

patinettes
pah-tee-<u>net</u>

самокаты
sah-mah-<u>kah</u>-tee

patinetes
pah-tee-<u>neh</u>-tehs

When boys and girls,
Mothers and fathers
get hungry in the park
In New York   or Paris,

Moscow   or Madrid
                          They eat . . .

soda	candy
citronnade	**bonbon**
see-troh-<u>nahd</u>	bohng-bohng
ситро	*конфеты*
<u>see</u>-troh	kohn-f'<u>yeh</u>-tee
limonada	**bombón**
lee-moh-<u>nah</u>-dah	bohm-<u>bohn</u>

pretzels	ice cream
bretzels	**glace**
bret-<u>sehl</u>	glahs
бублички	**мороженое**
<u>boob</u>-lee-chkee	mah-<u>roh</u>-zheh-nah-yeh
galletas	**helado**
gal-<u>yeh</u>-tahs	eh-<u>lah</u>-doh

When the day is gone
And everyone is tired

Fathers and mothers,
Sisters and brothers
Get ready to go home.

Everyone looks forward
To the next outing
In the park
In New York   or Paris,

Moscow   or Madrid.

Additional Words

boys	**garçons** gahr-<u>sohng</u>	**мальчики** mah'l-chee-kee	**muchachos** moo-<u>chah</u>-chohs
brother	**frère** frare	**брат** braht	**hermano** ehr-<u>mah</u>-noh
day	**jour** zhoor <small>zh = the sound of s in pleasure</small>	**день** d'yen	**día** <u>dee</u>-ah
father	**papa** pah-<u>pah</u>	**папа** <u>pah</u>-pah	**papá** pah-<u>pah</u>
fun	**amusement** ah-mewz-<u>mahng</u>	**удовольствие** oo-dah-<u>vohl</u>-stvee-yeh	**diversión** dee-vehr-see-<u>ohn</u>
girls	**filles** fee	**девочки** d'<u>yeh</u>-vah-ch'kee	**muchachas** moo-<u>chah</u>-chahs
good-by	**au revoir** ohr'<u>vwahr</u>	**до свиданья** doh svee-<u>dah</u>-n'yah	**adiós** ah-d'<u>yoss</u>
home	**maison** meh-<u>zohng</u>	**домой** dah-<u>moy</u>	**casa** <u>kah</u>-sah

English	French	Russian	Spanish
Madrid	**Madrid** mah-dreed	Мадрид mah-d'reed	**Madrid** mah-dreed
Moscow	**Moscou** mohs-koo	Москва mahs-k'vah	**Moscú** mohs-koo
mother	**maman** mah-mahng	мама mah-mah	**mamá** mah-mah
New York	**New York** new york	Нью Йорк new york	**Nueva York** nweh-vah york
outing	**excursion** ex-kewr-s'yohng	прогулка prah-gool-kah	**paseo** pah-seh-oh
Paris	**Paris** pah-ree	Париж pah-ree'zh	**París** pah-rees
park	**parc** pahrk	парк pahrk	**parque** pahr-keh
sister	**soeur** suhr	сестра s'yeh-strah	**hermana** ehr-mah-nah
visit	**visiter** vee-zee-teh	посещать pah-s'yeh-shchat'	**visitar** vee-see-tahr
zoo	**jardin zoologique** zhahr-dehng zoh-oh-loh-zheek	зоопарк zoh-oh-pahrk	**parque zoológico** pahr-keh thoh-oh-loh-hee-koh

Russian Alphabet

А а	ah as in arch		П п	p as in pie
Б б	b as in boy		Р р	r as in porridge
В в	v as in voice		С с	s as in stay
Г г	g as in good		Т т	t as in toy
Д д	d as in do		У у	oo as in foot
Е е	yeh as in yet		Ф ф	f as in fix
Ё ё	yoh as in yoyo		Х х	kh as in hot
Ж ж	zh as in pleasure		Ц ц	ts as in let's go
З з	z as in zero		Ч ч	ch as in church
И и	ee as in feet		Ш ш	sh as in short
Й й	y as in yeast		Щ щ	shch as in borshch
К к	k as in keep		Ъ ъ	separation sign (')
Л л	l as in luck		Ы ы	ih as in a drawn-out is
М м	m as in me		Ь ь	soft sign (preceding consonant pronounced as if ee followed)
Н н	n as in now			
О о	oh as in often when stressed, closer to ah when unstressed		Э э	eh as in empty
			Ю ю	yuh as you
			Я я	yah as in yard

DATE DUE